# THE Grand Slam COLLECTION

## Have Fun Collecting Baseball Cards

Jerry Ford

Lerner Publications Company ● Minneapolis

*To Marty, Maggie, and Louis. Thanks for your patience.
And to young collectors everywhere.*
                                    -JF

Front cover photo by Colleen Sexton
Back cover photo by Lori Schatschneider, courtesy
of Jim Kelly

*This book is available in two editions:*
Library binding by Lerner Publications Company
Soft cover by First Avenue Editions
241 First Avenue North
Minneapolis, MN 55401

Library of Congress Cataloging-in-Publication Data

Ford, Jerry, 1949-
    The grand slam collection : have fun collecting baseball cards / by
Jerry Ford.
        p.   cm. — (Collecting made easy)
    Includes index.
    Summary: Includes a brief history of baseball cards and
information on how to shop for, evaluate, buy, and preserve these
collectibles.
    ISBN: 0-8225-2350-7 (lib. bdg.)
    ISBN: 0-8225-9598-2 (pbk.)
    1. Baseball cards—Collectors and collecting—United States—
Juvenile literature. [1. Baseball cards—Collectors and collecting.]
I. Title. II. Series.
GV875.3.F67   1992
769'.49796357'0973—dc20                                91-34349
                                                            CIP
                                                            AC

Manufactured in the United States of America

1  2  3  4  5  6  7  8  9  10  01  00  99  98  97  96  95  94  93  92

# Contents

# Introduction

Five boys huddle in a corner. A few feet away, crowds of kids and adults shuffle along and peer at baseball cards stacked high on tables. The boys, however, don't notice the crowds.

Each boy is more interested in his own handful of cards and in a magazine-sized booklet full of price lists.

They are negotiating a deal. One boy offers a 1988 Topps Don Mattingly, a card worth about $1 if it's in mint condition. Another boy says that he'll give a Fleer 1987 Alan Trammell, worth only about 25 cents, for the Mattingly.

Could this be an even trade? Would you agree to it? Would you even know how to decide whether it was fair?

As it turns out, this deal might not be bad. The Trammell card is in truly mint condition. (It has been kept safe in a sealed plastic holder.) The Mattingly card has a bent corner that reduces its value.

How many people collect baseball cards? No one really knows. Card collecting is great partly because it's so informal. A small group of friends with only a few dollars can have as much fun as the big-money dealers. Fathers and mothers can trade with their kids. Even all by yourself you can enjoy building a collection of your favorite big-league players.

But when this colorful hobby goes big-time, it can get wild. Some card shows draw thousands of people and fill whole auditoriums. One Wall Street investment firm estimates that sales of new baseball cards by the five major card companies have recently totaled 3 billion cards and $350 million each year. And that doesn't even count all the money collectors have spent on *old* cards.

But let's step back from the big money for a minute. How is that Mattingly–Trammell deal going?

"Don't trade for the Mattingly. He's having a bad year," a third boy advises. "It's not worth it."

The boy with the Trammell card gives that some thought. Trammell is off to a superb start, and his baseball card has been rising in value each month, according to the baseball-card guides. He decides to take back his offer to trade Trammell for Mattingly.

But Mattingly is still trade bait. Almost immediately, another deal comes up.

"I'll take the '88 Mattingly and the pick of your cards for Mike Greenwell of Boston," another boy says.

The boy with the Mattingly card shuffles through his cards and pulls out a John Tudor card. After double-checking the price guide, he asks, "How about Mattingly and Tudor for Greenwell?"

"Deal!"

This 1951 cereal box offered a bonus — cards featuring sports heroes. The cards were printed right on the box.

# The Big Five **and** More
## A Quick History

First it was the tobacco companies. Then it was the candy and gum companies. Even cereal companies and other food companies got into the act.

The business of issuing baseball cards is more than 100 years old. The earliest cards were distributed by cigarette companies as a promotion in the 1880s. Since then, companies peddling many different products have used baseball cards as a sales tool. To get you to buy their gum instead of a competitor's gum, for example, a company might put a card in the gum package as a bonus. Somewhere along the line, however, baseball cards quit being just a bonus. They became the final product.

By the early 1990s, five major card companies — called the Big Five — dominated the market. Topps, Fleer, Donruss, Upper Deck, and Score were producing almost all the new baseball cards on the market.

Each of the card-producing companies pays a fee and is licensed — given permission — by Major League Baseball and the Major League Baseball Players Association to reproduce baseball cards. Major League Baseball grants the right to reproduce a team logo (the symbol associated with each team, such as the St. Louis Cardinals' red bird). And it is the Major League Baseball Players Association that licenses card companies to reproduce the images of players.

These card companies are very competitive businesses — as competitive as the players on the cards. They try to figure out what hobbyists and collectors want, and then the companies try to provide it. That's why each company produces so many different types of cards.

It's also why the card companies emphasize attractive designs and colors. Cards 100 years ago featured simple photographs or even drawings. Modern cards are slick, sophisticated, and colorful. To sell more cards, a company might drop a feature that has been around for years or even head off in a totally new direction.

But it hasn't always been that way. To understand modern baseball cards, let's take a quick trip back through time to see how a novelty became big business.

Tobacco companies started it all by adding baseball cards to packs of cigarettes. The cigarette packs were soft, so a piece of cardboard was inserted to stiffen the pack. Someone got an idea: Why not print pictures on this cardboard to attract customers? Pictures of baseball players were printed on some of these cards.

A New York-based cigarette company, Goodwin and Company, produced the first major issue of baseball cards in the mid-1880s. Until 1890 Goodwin issued more than 2,000 baseball cards with cigarette brands such as Gypsy Queen and Old Judge. Other cigarette companies distributed baseball cards with such cigarette brands as Virginia Brights, Kalamazoo Bats, and Cut Plugs. People paid a nickel for 10 cigarettes and a posed "action" photo of a baseball player on a card that measured 1.5 inches by 2.5 inches (about 3.75 centimeters by 6.25 centimeters).

An artist's view of a baseball game in the 1880s. Even in these early years, baseball cards were used to help sell products.

# The Honus Wagner Card

This Honus Wagner card is the rarest of all the baseball cards. Produced by Sweet Caporal Tobacco Company in 1909-11, the card was recalled when Wagner, who did not smoke, objected to the use of his picture in connection with a tobacco product. This is the prestige card among collectors.

Donated by Barry Halper.

A card with a special place in history. The National Baseball Library in Cooperstown, New York, preserves a Honus Wagner card in a sealed display case.

In 1890 the American Tobacco Trust was formed by a merger of all the large American tobacco companies. This killed competition in the cigarette business, so the need for promotional giveaways such as baseball cards ended. By 1895, American Tobacco had stopped using baseball cards as a promotion.

For a few years after that, cigarette packs without bonus cards were the rule. Then the rise of some small new tobacco companies and a court ruling against American Tobacco brought competition back to the industry. Tobacco companies revived baseball cards early in the 20th century.

The most valuable baseball card of all time came out of this era—the Honus Wagner card issued with Sweet Caporal cigarettes. Only a few Wagner cards were distributed after Wagner objected to appearing on a card associated with cigarettes. In 1991 Bruce McNall (the owner of the Los Angeles Kings hockey team) and hockey superstar Wayne Gretzky paid $451,000 to buy one of these cards.

The onset of World War I in 1914 stopped production of tobacco-company baseball cards. Candy and gum companies and bakeries became the major baseball-card producers. The producers of Cracker Jack, who issued cards as early as 1914, were among them. Cards were produced throughout the Great Depression until World War II, when shortages of paper and glue halted card production altogether.

This period between the wars produced some interesting cards, especially the introductory set of cards issued by the Goudey Gum Company in 1933. This set contains numerous Hall of Fame players (such as Babe Ruth). The National Chicle Gum Company produced Diamond Stars, another significant set that is popular with collectors of Depression-era cards.

In 1948—after World War II—the Bowman Gum Company and the Leaf Gum Company both released sets of baseball cards. (Bowman, operating under the name of "Gum, Inc.," had issued its first set even earlier, in 1939.) At this time, the right to use players' pictures on cards became a big issue. After arguing with Bowman over such rights, Leaf decided to drop out of the baseball-card business. Bowman was therefore the only major producer of baseball cards until the Topps Company came along in 1951.

The set Topps issued in 1951 (called Blue Backs and Red Backs because of their color) offered an interesting feature. Collectors could actually use the cards to play a game of baseball and keep score. Each card carried the name of a baseball play — single, double, ball, strike, double play, and so on. Kids could form teams, shuffle the cards, and deal out plays to each other as if the dealer were a pitcher delivering the ball to a batter.

In 1952 Topps issued a 407-card set. If you want to buy one, it will probably cost you more than any other set issued since World War II — about $52,000 for a mint-condition set. Why so pricey? This set contains the first Topps baseball cards of New York Yankee great Mickey Mantle and San Francisco star Willie Mays.

This 1952 set signaled trouble for Bowman. Although Bowman continued to produce cards through 1955, Topps was clearly on the rise. In 1956 Topps bought the Bowman Company and became the undisputed ruler of the baseball-card world.

Topps issued deckle-edged cards in 1969 and again in 1974. (This Willie Mays card is from 1969.) The wavy edges and the black-and-white photo give the card a homey look. The "signature" is not an autograph; the factory printed it on the card.

Some cards from the famous 1952 set by Topps. With this set, Topps became a major player in the baseball-card business. A few years later, Topps would dominate the field.

Despite its dominance, Topps tried a lot of new approaches to attract customers to their packets of gum, each pack containing five baseball cards. These novelties included a set in which each card had a piece of a puzzle printed on the back. If you collected the entire set, you could flip all the cards over and put them together to form a picture of a Major League player. Another gimmick, issued in 1965, was the "tattoo card." You could transfer an image of a player or the emblem of a team onto a moistened hand or arm by pressing the ink of the card against it.

Topps dominated the baseball-card market without any major competition for nearly 30 years. Other companies issued small sets of cards featuring former baseball greats (such as Fleer's 1959 Ted Williams set), but Topps was the only company making large sets of cards showing currently active players. Agreements with the players gave Topps the right to use their images.

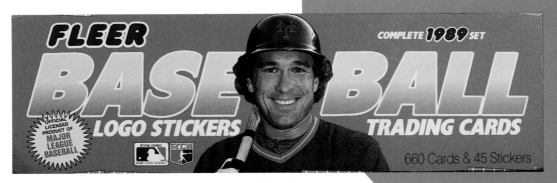

Notice the official seals below the words, "logo stickers." These seals indicate that the producer of this set has obtained permission—from both Major League Baseball and the Major League Baseball Players Association—to print team logos and pictures of players on these cards.

Other card companies, notably Fleer, challenged Topps and its control of the baseball-card market, but not very successfully. In 1963, when Fleer issued cards of current players and sold them along with a cookie, Topps won a court order against Fleer. The court said that Fleer could not issue such cards. Nobody, it seemed, could break the Topps stranglehold on the market.

Fleer finally got a court ruling against Topps in 1980. Although this ruling won Fleer almost no money, it turned out to be a landmark decision. The court declared that companies other than Topps should be allowed to buy photo-reproduction rights from baseball players. First Donruss, then Fleer, then other companies rushed to buy such rights.

A new era of competition began, and things have never been the same for card collectors. Baseball cards became a serious business. Special features were added. Traded sets—which feature players traded during the season—and other updated sets were introduced. Special rookie-card sets gave the hobbyist even more new cards to collect.

*(Opposite page)* This mint-condition rookie card (1989) for Ken Griffey, Jr., has a hologram on the back to identify it as a genuine Upper Deck product.

With so many new cards in this competitive market, collectors needed price guides to help them assess the values of cards. Magazines such as *Baseball Cards* and *Beckett Baseball Card Monthly* began surveying card prices and publishing price lists.

Meanwhile, even more card companies got into the act. In 1988 Score baseball cards entered the market—in a big way. Only three years later, Score produced the largest collector set ever released by a baseball-card company—900 cards.

The company that produces Score cards had earlier issued an unusual type of card. Sportflics "action cards,"

first issued in 1986, have a double image built into the front of the card. Held at one angle, a Sportflics card reveals one image, but a second image appears when the card is tilted at another angle.

Upper Deck is the newest big player in the trading-card business. Some collectors consider Upper Deck the "Cadillac of the card industry." Upper Deck's cards first came out in 1989 and were an immediate hit with collectors. Impressive graphics, a glossy finish, a high grade of paper, and even a hologram (a "three-dimensional" image made by laser) to prevent counterfeiting gave Upper Deck instant recognition among collectors.

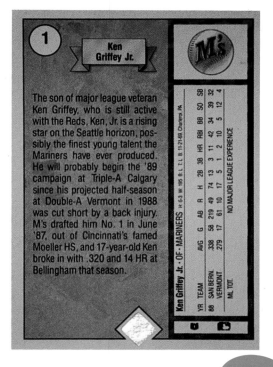

A huge selection of cards is available in wax packs at nearly any grocery store. You can't see through the wrapping of the pack, so you take your chances on getting the cards you want.

Besides the major card producers, other companies also turn out special issues of cards. You might find a special baseball-card offer at a fast-food restaurant, at a convenience store, or even in your daily newspaper. Some of these special cards are produced in cooperation with one of the Big Five card producers, but others are not.

With so many cards available, a card hobbyist can easily get confused. Very few collectors can keep track of every new issue of cards. Even fewer collectors can afford to buy every new card. Collectors have to make some choices. Instead of buying every card they want, most collectors focus on finding the special cards that they want the most. Then they have fun hunting for bargains. For many collectors, this search for just the right card at just the right price is half the fun of the hobby.

DREAM TEAM

SCORE®

FRANK VIOLA • P

# An *Endless* Set of **Sets**

The Big Five card companies (and other producers as well) issue most of their cards in sets. Instead of putting out one card at a time, these companies make a large group of cards available all at the same time. Each card in one of these sets has something in common with all of the other members of the set.

Part of the fun of collecting anything —and especially baseball cards—is in trying to get complete sets. The search for a few missing cards can be exciting. A special satisfaction comes with filling the last few gaps in an almost-complete set.

The collector certainly has enough sets to work with. There are regular sets, sealed factory sets, updated sets, traded sets, rookie sets—and a whole league of subsets within these larger sets.

An updated set from Fleer and a traded set from Topps—just a tiny sample of the many kinds of sets available to collectors

To clear up some of this confusion, here is a brief guide to the major types of sets:

**Regular Set**—A company's basic group of cards for a given year. This set, which is probably the largest set the company will issue all year, usually comes out early in the year.

**Sealed Factory Set**—Any complete set packaged by the manufacturer and still in its original wrapping.

**Updated Set**—A set that comes out late in the year and shows roster changes—new teams, new players, traded players, etc.—that have occurred since the regular set was issued.

**Traded Set**—A type of updated set that concentrates on players who have changed teams since the regular set was issued.

**Rookie Set**—A set that focuses on players in their first Major League season.

Some sets are very large—a regular set will probably contain several hundred cards—and others are very small. How can you know the number of cards you need to complete a set?

In many sets, the cards are numbered. If a line on the card says, for example, "211 of 660," you know that this card comes from a set of 660 cards. Your card is the 211th card in the set. Other sets, however, are not numbered. Even more confusing, some sets—especially some older ones like the 1933 Goudey set—are numbered incorrectly!

To keep track of how many cards are really in a set, you could consult one of the major card guides or a collector's magazine. Even if it takes a little research to find out how many cards a set should contain, most collectors want to know. They enjoy building full sets and hunting down the hard-to-find cards they need.

To start building your own set, buy a few wax packs (small packs of cards) at a supermarket, drugstore, or bookstore near you. Then open the packs and see what you've got. Until you open a wax pack, you never really know which cards you are buying. (The wrapping of the pack keeps you from seeing what's inside.) But no matter which cards you get, you have started building a set.

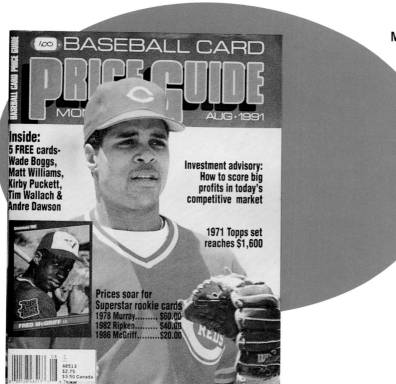

Monthly magazines like this one (from Krause Publications) are great sources of detailed information about baseball cards. They can tell you a lot besides average recent prices — including the number of cards that a complete set should include.

A trading session with a friend might bring you closer to completing a set. Try trading away your unwanted duplicates for the cards you still don't have.

As you buy more wax packs of a certain type of card, you will add to your set. Pretty soon you might find, for example, that you have all but 10 cards of a 44-card subset. You will probably also find that you have two, or three, or even four copies of a single card. Those extra cards are valuable. They will be your trade bait, the cards you give to other collectors in exchange for the cards you still need.

Building a set from scratch can be slow and tedious, but it can also be a lot more fun than just buying a complete factory set from a card dealer or hobby shop.

Not so long ago, you could not have bought a full factory set of cards even if you had wanted to. There weren't any. A collector had to buy many pieces of gum, or many cookies, or many of something else in order to get many cards. The companies who made the cards were trying to sell those other products, not the cards themselves.

Some regular sets were not even issued all at once. Topps, for example, issued its 407-card 1952 set in six parts—each part at a different time during the season. Not until 1974 did Topps begin selling its entire regular set of baseball cards all at once.

A sealed factory set is more valuable than a "hand-collated" set—a set made by getting a few cards at a time until the set is complete. All of the cards in a factory set will be in great condition. The factory guarantees it. If you are more interested in a set as an investment than as a source of trading fun, a factory set might be for you—if you can afford one.

Even hand-collated sets can be very expensive if you want to buy complete sets. Some of them are very large—containing several hundred cards. Even if a set doesn't contain any rare or unusual cards, the basic cost of so many cards is substantial.

Many factors other than size affect a set's value. For one thing, if it's not complete, it's not truly a set. Even one missing card is a major blow to a set's value. For another thing, a set with a few stained or worn-out cards will be worth much less than a set in near mint condition.

Maybe this box contains a complete 1989 Donruss set, maybe it doesn't. Because the plastic wrap has been removed from the box, anyone could easily take out a couple of cards.

The players represented in a set also make a big difference. Even one player can drive up the cost of a set of cards. A complete, near mint-condition, 1983 Topps regular set (792 cards) would probably cost you between $135 and $165. The much smaller Topps traded set from the same year and in similar condition—only 132 cards—would probably cost you slightly more than $100. Why? The traded set contains the rookie card of Darryl Strawberry (formerly of the New York Mets and later with the Los Angeles Dodgers)—a card that's worth almost $100 all by itself.

(NOTE: The card prices we give in this book are just for comparison. Prices change almost daily. Check a recent price-guide magazine for up-to-date values. Except where we specify some other condition for a card, any card value mentioned in this book will be for a card in near mint condition. See Chapter 9 for an explanation of card conditions.)

Similarly, Fleer's 660-card regular 1984 set sells for less than $200. Fleer's 132-card 1984 updated set, however, would probably go for nearly $500 because of three players. Boston Red Sox pitcher Roger Clemens, Minnesota Twins outfielder Kirby Puckett, and New York Mets pitcher Dwight Gooden all had rookie cards in the updated set. Each of these superstar rookie cards alone would probably cost you about $100.

Minnesota Twins outfielder Kirby Puckett. His rookie card is one of the high-value items in Fleer's 1984 updated set.

# TOPPS Baseball CHECK LIST
## 475 SIXTH SERIES

| | | | | | | | |
|---|---|---|---|---|---|---|---|
| 441 | J. Marshall | 449 | G. Fodge | 458 | J. Becquer | 467 | G. Hobbie |
| 442 | P. Paine | 450 | P. Ward | 459 | R. Blackburn | 468 | B. Schmidt |
| 443 | B. Harrell | 451 | J. Taylor | 460 | C. Essegian | 469 | D. Ferrarese |
| 444 | D. Kravitz | 452 | R. Mejias | 461 | E. Mayer | 470 | R. C. Stevens |
| 445 | B. W. Smith | 453 | T. Qualters | 462 | G. Geiger | 471 | L. Green |
| 446 | C. Hardy | 454 | H. Hanebrink | 463 | V. Valentinetti | 472 | J. Jay |
| 447 | R. Monzant | 455 | H. Griggs | 464 | C. Flood | 473 | B. Renna |
| 448 | C. Lau | 456 | D. Brown | 465 | A. Portocarrero | 474 | R. Semproch |
| | | 457 | M. Pappas | 466 | P. Whisenant | | |

## SPORT MAGAZINE ALL STAR SELECTION for 1958

| | | | | | | | |
|---|---|---|---|---|---|---|---|
| 475 | Haney & Stengel | 479 | N. Fox | 485 | T. Williams | 491 | S. Lollar |
| 476 | S. Musial | 480 | E. Mathews | 486 | W. Mays | 492 | B. Friend |
| 477 | B. Skowron | 481 | F. Malzone | 487 | M. Mantle | 493 | B. Turley |
| 478 | J. Temple | 482 | E. Banks | 488 | H. Aaron | 494 | W. Spahn |
| | | 483 | L. Aparicio | 489 | J. Jensen | 495 | H. Score |
| | | 484 | F. Robinson | 490 | E. Bailey | | |

One of the checklist cards for a 1958 Topps set. Even though they are not as flashy as regular cards, checklist items are still an important part of the set.

Collectors who build sets by hand should never throw away any part of a set—even if it seems to have no value. Of course, every player card is worth something. Even a seemingly useless card might help you make a trade. Also, you never know when a previously boring player will become a big star. Put a guy in the World Series, let him hit a couple of home runs, and watch the value of his card skyrocket.

Sometimes a set will contain things other than player cards. These pieces are also important. For example, some Topps sets contained checklist cards—cards that just list the other cards in the set. Because the checklist cards look so unusual—no picture, no featured player—some collectors simply threw them away. Wrong! In fact, so many people threw these checklists away that they have become rarer and more valuable than the player cards in the set. For example, one of the two checklist cards from the 1956 Topps set would probably cost you more than $220.

The Donruss "Diamond Kings" subset features artistic portraits of selected players. If you buy wax packs of Donruss cards, you might find a "Diamond Kings" card mixed in with cards of the regular set.

Never, ever purchase a hand-collated set of cards without inspecting the contents. Know which cards should be in the set, and ask the seller to let you look through it. If the seller won't allow it, walk away. If the seller does let you flip through the cards, search not only for the most expensive cards but for every card. Make sure they are all there. After all, when you buy a set, you pay extra for completeness.

Many card companies issue special subsets—small groups of cards focusing on one type of player. (These subsets are usually included with the factory set.) Donruss, for example, selects one player every year from each of the Major League teams and honors these players as "Diamond Kings." Each selected player appears on a special card that features a painting instead of a photograph. Donruss includes this 26-card Diamond King subset as part of its basic factory set. The company also includes another subset, "Rated Rookies," in its basic factory set each year to honor the top rookies coming into the majors that year.

Topps includes subsets such as "Record Breakers," "All-Stars," and a feature called "Turn Back the Clock" in its factory sets. Score offers a "Dream Team" subset (featuring the top players in the game), another focusing on the World Series, and another highlighting top draft choices by Major League teams—all subsets included in the factory-issued set. Fleer includes a "Rookie Prospects" subset and other special commemorative cards in its factory set.

The fun of collecting begins with your first efforts to build a full set. It grows as you complete one set, then two, then more. When you fill that last gap in a set, you will feel the sense of accomplishment that inspires collectors to build set after set after set.

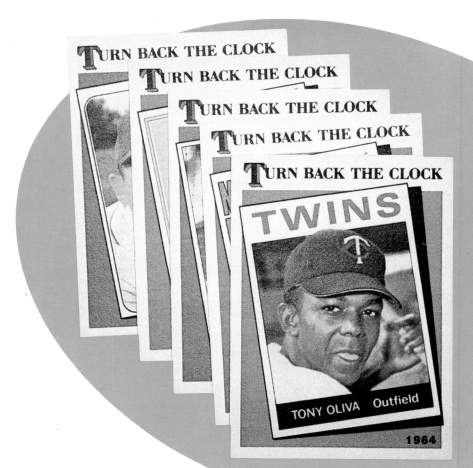

Tony Oliva, a master at the plate during the 1960s, was still making it onto baseball cards 25 years later. He was one of the players included in the 1989 "Turn Back the Clock" subset by Topps.

**3**

Before the start of the 1991 season, Chuck Knoblauch was just a rookie on a last-place team. By the following November, he was a World Series star and the American League's Rookie of the Year. Collectors who had stocked up on this Upper Deck rookie card for Knoblauch were all smiles.

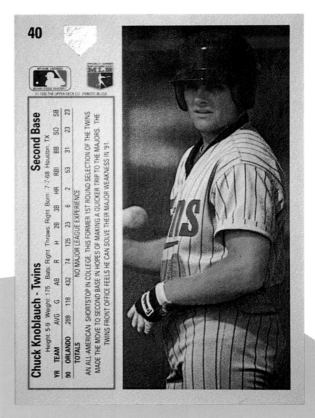

| YR | TEAM | AVG | G | AB | R | H | 2B | 3B | HR | RBI | BB | SO | SB |
|----|------|-----|---|----|---|---|----|----|----|-----|----|----|----|
| 90 | ORLANDO | .289 | 118 | 432 | 74 | 125 | 23 | 6 | 2 | 53 | 31 | 23 | 23 |
| | TOTALS | | | | | | | | | | | | |

NO MAJOR LEAGUE EXPERIENCE

AN ALL-AMERICAN SHORTSTOP IN COLLEGE, THIS FORMER 1ST ROUND SELECTION OF THE TWINS MADE THE MOVE TO SECOND BASE IN HOPES OF MAKING A QUICKER TRIP TO THE MAJORS. THE TWINS FRONT OFFICE FEELS HE CAN SOLVE THEIR MAJOR WEAKNESS IN '91.

Chuck Knoblauch - Twins
Second Base
Height: 5-9 Weight: 175 Bats: Right Throws: Right Born: 7-7-68 Houston, TX

40

# New Cards on the Block
## Rookie Cards

It happens to most baseball-card collectors. They look at a rookie and see something special. The player hits a towering home run and the collector starts believing that this guy is the next Babe Ruth. The collector, stricken with "rookie fever," buys up every available rookie card for this budding superstar.

A rookie card *is* special. It is a player's first-year card, so it carries with it the hope of a career about to take off. The rookie card is often the rarest and most valuable of all a player's cards. It is made even more valuable if only one card company has issued a rookie card for the player.

Ken Griffey, Jr., of the Seattle Mariners. Griffey's rookie card from Upper Deck was worth a great deal of money only one year after it was issued.

Most first-year cards take years to rise in value. Before card collecting became big business, a rookie card's value never went through the roof overnight. People who kept those cards, however, saw some faster action later on. Consider one classic rookie card, the 1952 Topps card for Mickey Mantle. If you want one in mint condition, you'll have to pay at least $7,500 for it. In one year alone, from 1989 to 1990, the value of that card increased by $1,000. The prices of a few modern rookie cards have skyrocketed right away. One good example is the 1989 Upper Deck rookie card for Ken Griffey, Jr. —worth $10 (in mint condition) at the end of the 1989 season but selling for about $55 two years later.

Even though rookie cards are interesting, why would a collector snap up every available rookie card for a player? The collector who buys cards this way is speculating—buying low-priced cards in the hope that their value will rise. The collector doesn't really want to own 58 rookie cards for one player. He or she wants to keep one or two and sell the rest for a lot more than the original price.

Speculation is risky. No one knows for sure which rookies will become stars and which ones will eventually keep benches warm in minor-league dugouts. Consequently, nobody really knows which cards will rise in value. Many collectors, however, find it exciting to try picking future superstars.

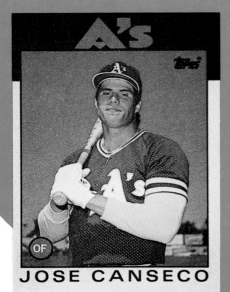

JOSE CANSECO

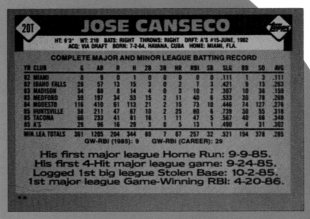

The card back reads:

### JOSE CANSECO  20T

HT: 6'3" WT: 210 BATS: RIGHT THROWS: RIGHT DRFT: A'S #15-JUNE, 1982
ACQ: VIA DRAFT BORN: 7-2-64, HAVANA, CUBA HOME: MIAMI, FLA.

**COMPLETE MAJOR AND MINOR LEAGUE BATTING RECORD**

| YR | CLUB | G | AB | R | H | 2B | 3B | HR | RBI | SB | SLG | BB | SO | AVG |
|---|---|---|---|---|---|---|---|---|---|---|---|---|---|---|
| 82 | MIAMI | 8 | 9 | 0 | 1 | 0 | 0 | 0 | 0 | 0 | .111 | 1 | 3 | .111 |
| 82 | IDAHO FALLS | 28 | 57 | 13 | 15 | 3 | 0 | 2 | 7 | 3 | .421 | 9 | 13 | .263 |
| 83 | MADISON | 34 | 88 | 8 | 14 | 4 | 0 | 3 | 10 | 2 | .307 | 10 | 38 | .159 |
| 83 | MEDFORD | 59 | 197 | 34 | 53 | 15 | 2 | 11 | 40 | 6 | .533 | 30 | 78 | .269 |
| 84 | MODESTO | 116 | 410 | 61 | 113 | 21 | 2 | 15 | 73 | 10 | .446 | 74 | 127 | .276 |
| 85 | HUNTSVILLE | 58 | 211 | 47 | 67 | 10 | 2 | 25 | 80 | 6 | .739 | 30 | 55 | .318 |
| 85 | TACOMA | 60 | 233 | 41 | 81 | 16 | 1 | 11 | 47 | 5 | .567 | 40 | 66 | .348 |
| 85 | A'S | 29 | 96 | 16 | 29 | 3 | 0 | 5 | 13 | 1 | .490 | 4 | 31 | .302 |
| MIN. LEA. TOTALS | | 361 | 1205 | 204 | 344 | 69 | 7 | 67 | 257 | 32 | .521 | 194 | 378 | .285 |

GW-RBI (1985): 9    GW-RBI (CAREER): 29

His first major league Home Run: 9-9-85.
His first 4-Hit major league game: 9-24-85.
Logged 1st big league Stolen Base: 10-2-85.
1st major league Game-Winning RBI: 4-20-86.

JOSE CANSECO

Anyone who picked Jose Canseco of the Oakland A's back in 1986 sure guessed right. Canseco has reached superstar status—on the field *and* with collectors. Both Donruss and Fleer issued Canseco rookie cards in their regular sets for the 1986 season. The more valuable of these is the Donruss card, which trades for about $110. The Fleer card is also worth a lot—but only about half of what the Donruss card is worth. One big reason for this is that the Donruss card features Canseco alone, while Canseco shares his Fleer rookie card with relief pitcher Eric Plunk.

Rookie cards can be too expensive for a lot of collectors. What can you do if you want a player in your collection but you can't afford his rookie card? Consider collecting second-year cards, often called "sophomore" cards. These are usually not as expensive as rookie cards, but they get you the players you want and still give you a piece of baseball history—at a price you can afford. For example, a mint-condition 1978 Topps rookie card for Alan Trammell of the Detroit Tigers would cost you about $50. Too steep? Try Trammell's sophomore card, which sells for about $10 in mint condition.

If that's still too expensive, then think about getting a third-year card. You can probably get Trammell's for about $5. You may later consider that a bargain if Trammell is elected to the Hall of Fame.

If second- or third-year cards are still too expensive, go for what you can afford. The 1967 Topps rookie card for former Minnesota Twin and California Angel Rod Carew, who was recently elected to the Hall of Fame, is worth about $475 in near mint condition. His second-year card is more affordable (about $13), but that may still stretch your budget. Carew's third-year card (1969) is worth under $9, but that's still a hefty price. You can, however, get Carew for about 30 cents if you can be happy with his 1986 Topps card.

Great beginnings do not mean a card will hold its value. For every Jose Canseco, there is a Matt Nokes or a Sam Horn.

This deckle-edged Topps card for Rod Carew was issued in 1969. A fine card with an interesting format, it might make a good acquisition for a collector who can't quite afford a Carew rookie card.

Nokes, a former catcher for Detroit, put together a strong rookie season in 1987 and set the record for the most home runs (32) hit by a rookie catcher. Horn slammed some gigantic homers in 1987 during his rookie season with the Boston Red Sox. After those early glory days, however, both fell on hard times. So did the value of their cards—to about one-tenth their peak value. Even though both seemed to be regaining their home-run ways in the early 1990s, how far will their cards rebound? It's hard to say for sure.

Card companies have even started trying to get a jump on hot careers by issuing minor-league cards. Before a player even makes it to the majors, he might have his picture on a baseball card. Cards like that can be interesting, but mostly as a side-show to the real baseball-card action. Buy them for fun, but don't plan on very many of your minor-league cards riding a player's career to the top of the market. The chance is very slim.

Rookie cards are always a gamble. Nobody knows which rookies will prove themselves in the big leagues. Still, you can have a bit of fun taking your best guess, investing a few dollars in rookie cards, and tracking your picks.

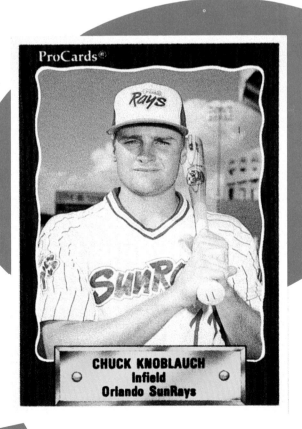

**And back to Knoblauch. Here's an unusual item—a minor-league card for someone who eventually *did* make it big. If you invested in a few of these cards before Knoblauch became a star, you have incredibly good luck.**

Hundreds of card collectors gathered at a card show in Minnesota to shop and to admire classic cards.

# *To* Drool Is Not *Cool*
## Baseball-Card Shows

A card show can be an awesome, emotional event for the first-time visitor. You will probably see some legendary cards, but remember — even if you're starstruck — to drool is not cool. That's just one of the many unwritten rules to follow at a card show.

In some ways, these shows are like traveling museums — perhaps your only chance to gaze upon a $1,200 Nolan Ryan rookie card, securely locked up in a glass case. Hobbyists gather at the shows to admire truly rare and expensive items. But a card show is also a place to do business. A serious shopper can find a great selection of cards all in one building.

Almost every town in North America hosts a card show now and then. All that's necessary is a big place — like a church basement, a school auditorium, or a shopping mall — where card vendors can set up tables and spread out their cards.

Boston Red Sox relief pitcher Jeff Reardon autographs cards at a show. When professional ballplayers give out autographs at a show, you might have to pay a higher admission fee.

Admission to many card shows is free. To get into others, you might have to pay a small fee (often only $1). If some major-league star is giving out autographs at the show, however, the admission fee could be a lot higher.

Once you're in the show, you are free to wander from one dealer's table to another. This is an excellent chance to talk to several card dealers and learn a few things about the cards you're interested in. Most dealers know a lot about their cards and are willing to offer advice to a young collector.

Each dealer's display will probably feature unusual cards or the classics that the dealer is most proud of. These might be very expensive. To cover their costs of being in the show—such as their table rent or their travel expenses—the dealers want to make good money in a short time. Still, every dealer will also have less costly cards for sale. Just ask.

Dealers are happy to show you what's for sale. Never touch any cards, however, unless the dealer gives you permission. One greasy finger can destroy an unprotected card. Also, be careful not to lean on tables or cases. You will not be a welcome customer if you knock over anyone's display.

If you do see a card you're interested in, don't be afraid to negotiate with a dealer. Many dealers ask slightly more for a card than they expect to get. You should make the dealer a low offer, and then you and the dealer can settle on a price somewhere between the asking price and your offer.

Know what a card should be worth. The price guides—such as the *Beckett Baseball Card Monthly* or *Baseball Cards*—can help give you a basic idea of a card's value. The price in the guide, however, is not carved in stone. Card prices go up and down every day. No guide can keep up with all these changes, so use your head.

And use your feet. If one dealer won't sell for the price you are willing to pay, go to a different table. Check out other dealers' prices. You can always go back to the first dealer if that price turns out to be the best. A smart buyer shops around.

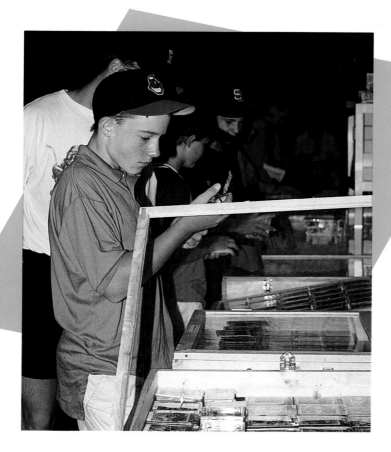

A dealer at a card show might open a display case to let customers look closely at what's for sale. Still, customers should never handle cards unless the dealer approves.

An advertisement in *Beckett Baseball Card Monthly* announces a major card show in Houston. Check these ads occasionally to see if a big show will be held near you.

To find out about a card show near you, try looking through the sports section of your local newspaper. You might find an advertisement for an upcoming show. Usually the shows are held on weekends, so check the newspaper a few days in advance. You should also check the classified ads in your paper. The price-guide magazines might also run an ad for a big show near you.

Are you friends with an experienced collector? Maybe he or she knows when and where the shows are held. Do you know of a good sports-card shop? (If you don't, try looking in the Yellow Pages of your phone book under "Sporting Goods," "Collectibles," or, in larger cities, "Baseball Cards.") The owners of these shops are often the first to know when a card show is coming to town. Some shops even post ads for upcoming shows.

Find a show and go! Just remember to be cool, keep your excitement under control, and have a great time.

When cards are traded outside the Metrodome in Minneapolis — the home field of the Minnesota Twins — cards of hometown players generate a lot of interest.

# Hot Bat, Hot Card?
## What Makes a Card Valuable?

How can you estimate a card's value? Why do some cards take off in price while others remain stagnant? The answers to these questions are not simple. Of course, a card's condition is very important, but that's a topic we'll cover later (see Chapter 9). Other things also matter.

One basic rule is that something rare but desirable will probably be expensive. Economists call this the "law of supply and demand." This "law" applies to baseball cards. When a lot of people want a certain card but not many copies are available, the value of that card will soar.

On-field performance can also affect the price of a player's card. For example, Cecil Fielder had been in baseball for a long time before his 1986 rookie card became very valuable. At the start of the 1990 season, Fielder was not very well known, and his rookie card sold for only about 25 cents. By the end of 1990, the very same card cost more than $6. Why? Because Fielder hit a league-leading 51 home runs for Detroit in 1990.

The opposite is also true. If a player's career looks like it's crashing, the value of his card will probably drop as well. All those people who bought truckloads of his rookie card will try to unload them fast—and will be willing to take a pretty modest price.

The value of a card also depends on where you buy it. In St. Louis, Fielder's rookie card might sell for $6, while outside the gates of Tiger Stadium in Detroit you might be able to sell the same card for $14. The closer you are to Fielder and his home stadium, the more interest there will be in one of his cards.

For many years, Cecil Fielder's 1986 rookie card from Topps caused very little excitement among collectors. Then, in 1990, Fielder slammed 51 home runs for the Detroit Tigers. As Fielder captured baseball's attention, his card rose rapidly in value.

BLUE JAYS

1B

CECIL FIELDER

Do you have a card that one of your friends really wants? If so, you might be able to get a good deal in a trade.

Sometimes a card's value rises just because a player strikes the fancy of the fans. Jose Canseco of the Oakland A's, for example, is a superb home-run hitter, but Fielder is at least as strong at the plate as Canseco is. Still, Canseco's rookie card from Donruss sells for about 10 times the price of a Fielder rookie card.

Finally, a card's value depends on the person who's buying it. Imagine a collector who needs only the rookie card of Minnesota's Chuck Knoblauch to complete a 1991 set. After weeks and weeks of searching, this frustrated collector finally sees the Knoblauch card in a dealer's display case. To this collector, a Knoblauch card is worth more than it would be to 99.9 percent of the other people on the planet. A smart dealer who senses this enthusiasm could get a pretty good price for that card from this buyer.

**6**

In 1989, Score's Ray Knight card came out with an embarrassing mistake — the photo was reversed. Score quickly issued a corrected version after the error was discovered. Which of these two cards is the error card? Try reading the word "Tigers" on the front of Knight's jersey.

# When *an* Error *Is* a *Hit*

Nobody is perfect—and that definitely includes the makers of baseball cards. Errors in the production of baseball cards—sometimes small mistakes, sometimes major goof-ups—make for some interesting stories. They might also dramatically increase the value of a card.

To understand this odd aspect of baseball-card collecting, you have to know a little bit about how cards are made. After each card company decides which players to include in its regular and special sets, artists design the front and back of each card. The company selects a photograph (or drawing) of each player to fit into the design. Researchers gather statistical information about each player to print on the back of the card. Then a writer puts it into words.

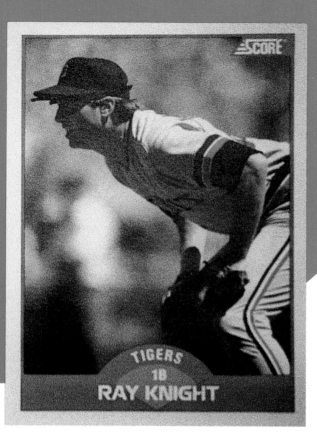

TIGERS
1B
RAY KNIGHT

All of this information is double-checked in reference books before the card gets printed. Also, the company checks to make sure that the proper photograph is used with each player's card.

That's a lot of work. And each of the big companies does this for hundreds of cards every year. Especially in the case of rookie cards, the company might have only a few weeks to go from idea to finished card. With so many people trying to bring together so many pictures and so many pieces of information so fast, there are countless chances to make a mistake.

It's amazing that mistakes in print are so rare. Collectors always notice the errors that do get printed, but we'll never know how many mistakes are prevented by proofreaders and editors in the card companies.

What kinds of errors can occur? Just about anything. Maybe a statistic will be incorrect. Even worse, maybe the photo will be reversed, making a left-handed batter, for example, appear to be a right-hander. Worse yet, maybe the wrong picture will go onto a card, so that the player in the photo turns out to be somebody other than the player named on the card.

When a major mistake occurs, the card company rushes to fix it. They can't do much about the cards that have already been printed and sold, but they can make sure that any future printings are without the error. Often a corrected card will be included in one of the company's sets issued later in the year, such as a traded set or an extended set.

Errors make the card unusual and interesting. Especially if the card company issues a corrected version of the card, an error card might also be quite rare. This combination of oddity and scarcity can make the error card more valuable than the corrected card.

For example, Donruss switched the backs of Nolan Ryan's regular 1990 card and the 1990 card honoring the Texas Ranger pitcher for surpassing the 5,000-strikeout mark. Donruss discovered the error and issued a new, corrected card. Collectors, however, started a bidding frenzy for the error card, which soon became worth as much as $15. Meanwhile, the corrected card was selling for about 75 cents.

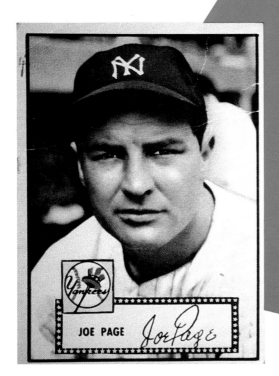

These are the corrected versions of the Joe Page and Johnny Sain cards from the 1952 Topps set. When cards for these two players first came out that year, Page's picture was on Sain's card and vice versa.

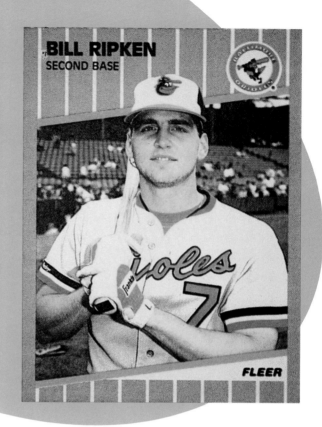

The Billy Ripken obscenity card from 1989 was one of the most famous — and embarrassing — baseball-card errors. Here is a version of the card with the obscenity blacked out.

Another famous error card is the 1989 Fleer card of Baltimore Oriole Billy Ripken. An obscenity clearly appeared on the handle of Ripken's bat. After the cards were printed, Fleer discovered the obscenity and tried several ways of getting rid of it. On some cards they used a white correction fluid. On others, they scribbled out the obscenity. Finally, Fleer blotted out the offensive wording with a black box.

Collectors now had four different versions of Billy Ripken's card to choose from: the uncensored profanity card, the white-blotched card, the scribbled card, and the black-box card. The original card — with the obscene word clearly visible — traded at some shows for as much as $150 for a while, but its selling price eventually came down to about $18. The version with the white correction fluid is the most valuable version, worth about $25. The scribbled card would probably cost you about $15, and the black-box card sells for only slightly more than $1.

One of the first famous errors came in the legendary Topps 1952 regular set. Johnny Sain's picture appears on Joe Page's card, and vice versa. One of these error cards in near mint condition would probably cost you about $300; Sain's corrected card would go for about $90 and Page's for less than $70.

By waiting until the end of a card show, this lucky customer found a half-price special on cards. Patience can pay off.

Some collectors have accused card companies of intentionally including errors in their cards, just to generate publicity. That's hard to believe. Companies spend a lot of money to correct error cards—probably a lot more than they make from increased sales.

Sales of an error card do increase soon after a mistake is discovered. The price of one of those cards is likely to skyrocket at that point. In almost all cases, however, the price of the error card falls later on. If you find an error card that you want to own, take it slow. Don't buy at the top of the price surge. Wait until the price drops and stays at a certain level for a while.

Even if you are pretty sure the price has bottomed out, you are still taking a risk. The price can always go lower. Therefore, you should never risk any money that you can't afford to lose. Have fun, but let the card companies make the errors.

**7**

Admitting to your friends that you paid too much for a card can be tough. Avoid costly mistakes by knowing what you want and how much it's worth.

# "I Can't Believe I Bought It!"

It's a horrible feeling. You wake up one morning and wonder why you let yourself get so excited at a card show, or at a store, or even just in a trading session with your friends. Your emotions ran away with you, and you bought—or traded for—cards you did not really want. Or maybe you wanted a certain card, but you say to yourself, "I can't believe I paid that much!"

You're not the first collector to feel that way. Eagerness to complete a set or buy a special card can lead even good collectors into some bad deals. To make this bad feeling a rare one, try setting goals and sticking with them. Do you want to make big profits? Are you mostly interested in completing a set? Do you want to have the largest collection in town?

A sample page from *Beckett Baseball Card Monthly*. Magazines like this come out frequently because card prices are constantly changing. Before you make a major purchase of cards, check the latest issue of one of these price guides.

If profit is your goal, you are not really a collector but a *speculator.* Just like a trader in the stock market, you want to buy something at a low price and sell it later at a higher price. You want the money the card can bring, not the card itself. There is nothing wrong with this attitude. Baseball cards can be valuable. Still, you should recognize that other people have different motives.

Collectors enjoy putting together and keeping a group of cards they really like. The collector is motivated by the desire to have the cards, not by money. Often collectors try to complete certain sets of cards. Sometimes collectors have lofty goals and can't be satisfied until they have more cards than anyone else they know.

No matter what your motives, make sure your goals are realistic. Don't expect to have the largest collection in the state if you earn only $5 a week mowing your neighbor's lawn. Baseball cards can be very expensive, and a big-time collector could easily spend several thousand dollars a year on cards.

Prices for a set of cards from Topps, Donruss, Fleer, Score, or Upper Deck range from $20 to $50. But those prices are only for the basic regular set. If you want all of the company's other sets—traded, rookie, extended, whatever—get ready to spend some major bucks.

Then there are the other cards. A major-league baseball park might put out its own set of cards featuring the home team. Hundreds of businesses, from hot-dog companies to convenience stores, issue special baseball cards. Charitable groups might also issue cards to raise money. With so many choices, you have to focus your buying.

First, set a budget. Allow yourself only a certain amount of money to spend on cards, and don't spend a penny more. Buy the best cards you can get for that amount.

A dealer at a card show will probably have a price guide close at hand. Both the seller and the buyer of a card want to know approximately what a card should cost.

Find the kinds of cards you like, and then concentrate on buying those. Maybe you want to fill out a set for a certain year. Some collectors concentrate on one company's cards because they like the design, or they trust the statistics, or they like the company's selection of players. Or maybe you want to collect cards for the players on a certain team, or the best players at a certain position, or even all of the Major Leaguers named Henry. Whatever. The goal is up to you. The important thing is to set one.

No matter what your goal is, keep these tips in mind:

♦ Start small. Every great collection starts with a few cards.
♦ Keep to your budget.
♦ Specialize. Focus on a certain type of card.
♦ Know what a fair price is for the cards you want.
♦ At a card show, shop around and negotiate.
♦ If you are a speculator, try to invest in cards of little-known players likely to have a great season.
♦ Build a good relationship with a local baseball-card dealer. Let the dealer help you find what you are looking for.

Your parents can help you set a budget for your card purchases. If you can't decide on a collecting goal, talk it out with your parents and your friends.

At a baseball-card shop, you can find valuable information as well as cards. A good relationship with an honest dealer is important to most experienced collectors.

# Who Can *You* Trust?

How can you tell whether the autograph on a baseball card is genuine? Unless you're a handwriting expert, you probably can't. Let's face it: a dishonest person trying to sell a forgery could fool most of us.

Fortunately, most baseball-card dealers are honest. They want to get a fair price for their cards, but they don't want to cheat you. Still, most serious card collectors are careful consumers. They check out every detail of a card before buying it. They also buy only from respected dealers who have been in business for a while.

Quality, trust, and honesty are crucial to any business, and that includes baseball-card shops. If dealers don't offer high-quality cards, if they mislead their customers, or if they price their merchandise too high, they won't stay in business very long. If a shop has survived for several years, it has probably been doing something right. Especially for a new collector, an established shop is a safe bet.

You may wonder how a card seller could cheat you. After all, you can see what you're buying before you buy it. How could anyone pull a fast one?

One common way is to disguise the true condition of a card. (See Chapter 9 for some tips on how to rate the condition of a card.) Fuzzy edges or drooping corners reduce a card's value, so some slimy characters have been known to shave off frayed edges. A shaved card might look pretty good, but it will be slightly smaller than it should be. An experienced collector would notice this, but someone new to card collecting might be tricked into paying too much for this damaged card.

A dishonest seller could also tamper with packages of cards and reduce the customer's chances of getting valuable items. Card companies package their cards in wax-pack combinations that mix popular, high-demand cards with less popular cards. If a dealer knew where the popular cards would be, he or she could remove them and replace them with less desirable cards. At one time, this was possible because the order of the cards was predictable. Card companies, however, have changed to less predictable packaging systems to reduce such tampering.

A dishonest card seller might shave fuzzy edges off a card to disguise its true condition. A shaved card has nice-looking edges, but it is slightly smaller than a normal card. This damage makes a card almost worthless.

Notice the shiny packages on the lower shelves of this display case. The plastic wrapping on these packages is like a factory-applied seal. If it's not broken, the cards in the package are almost certainly in mint condition.

Tampering with a sealed factory set is not easy. Even an inexperienced collector would notice a broken seal and become suspicious. Hand-collated sets, however—those put together by individual collectors—could contain almost anything. If you're buying a set other than a factory-sealed set, always make sure the set is complete and always check the condition of the cards.

Finally, don't be sucked in by promises of incredible bargains. Anyone selling or trading a card wants to do well in the transaction. Do you really believe that anyone would cheat himself or herself just to offer you a great deal? Remember: if something seems too good to be true, it probably is.

Again, most dealers are honest. By choosing your dealer carefully and by being an alert buyer, you can make sure that your card purchases are a source of fun, not frustration.

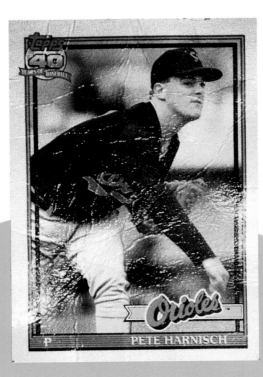

This 1991 Pete Harnisch card from Topps is not very old, but it looks like it's been through a few wars. Its condition: poor. Its value: zero.

# From Mint to Mutilation
## The Condition of Cards

Let's say you've got a 1980 Topps rookie card for Rickey Henderson. You want to sell it to me. How much would I be willing to pay?

That's a hard question to answer until I know the answer to another one: What condition is it in? Is it in near mint condition—almost perfect? If so, I might be willing to pay as much as $180 for it. Is it in excellent condition—with a few minor defects? If so, I wouldn't be willing to pay any more than $90. Is it in poor condition—

marred by a catastrophic defect? If so, I'll give you a dime for it.

Serious collectors know that cards with nicks, cuts, scrapes, or frayed edges are a lot less valuable than well-preserved cards. Even an inexperienced collector learns quickly about the faults that reduce a card's value. Although opinions about a card's condition might vary from one person to another, collectors do have some guidelines for describing a card's condition.

Monthly magazines that circulate nationally, such as *Beckett Baseball Card Monthly* (of Dallas, Texas) and *Baseball Cards* (of Iola, Wisconsin), have systems for rating the quality of baseball cards. These magazines then list average prices paid recently for cards in a wide range of conditions, from mint through poor.

To put together their price guides, these magazines survey hobbyists and dealers throughout the nation. They ask what prices customers and dealers are paying for various cards. After the results come in, the editors average out the prices to show where the middle of the price range is for a given card in a given condition.

Of course, these prices are not fixed. They represent only an average. Many buyers paid more than the average and many paid less. The guides, however, are still helpful to a collector. They help the hobbyist know immediately whether the price of a card is even close to where it should be. If it is, then the heavy negotiations for an exact price can begin.

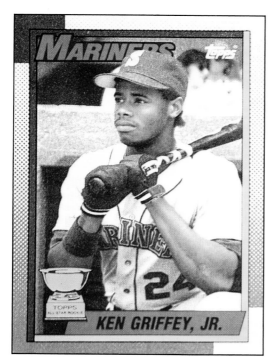 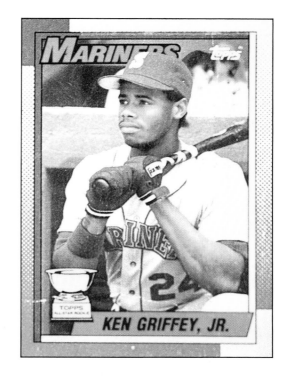

The card on the left is in mint condition. The card on the right, with its badly faded colors, is in poor condition. Because of the color difference, the card on the left is worth about nine times more than the card on the right.

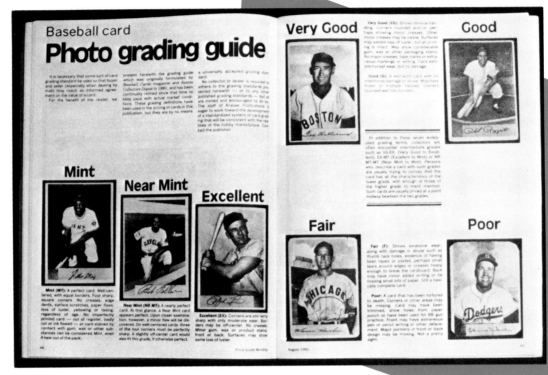

This guide to card photos appears in the *Price Guide Monthly,*
a magazine published by Krause Publications. Although rating cards
is not an exact science, guidelines such as these are accepted by most collectors.

Those negotiations will probably focus a lot on the quality of the card. The seller might claim that the card is in excellent condition, whereas the buyer might insist that it's only in very good condition. Such disagreements are possible because card rating is not an exact science.

Still, the guidelines used by the price-guide magazines are useful. The following is a summary of the card-rating scheme used by *Beckett Baseball Card Monthly:*

**Mint:** In perfect condition, with no defects from either printing or handling.

Unopened factory sets are considered in mint condition until the seal is broken on the set.

**Near Mint:** In nearly perfect condition. A card earning this rating has only a micro defect—some hard-to-see fault like very slightly fuzzy corners, loss of a small amount of original gloss, minor wear to the edges, or a little bit of discoloration along the borders. A micro defect is so small that it can be seen only under very close inspection. For a card to be classified in near mint condition, it can have no more than one micro defect.

**Excellent Mint:** Having several micro defects, but no minor defects. Again, these micro defects can be spotted only under very close inspection.

**Excellent:** Having some minor defects —such as slightly rounded corners, loss of original gloss, slightly worn edges, off-center borders, or off-white color.

**Very Good:** Having only one obvious major defect—like rounded corners, frayed edges or borders, loss of gloss from the surface of the card, or loss of color around the borders. Defects classified as "major" usually result from excessive handling.

**Good:** Having more than one major defect (such as loss of color, obvious signs of wear, rounded and frayed edges and corners, uneven color, or loss of surface gloss) but no catastrophic defects.

A card dealer at a show is careful to protect every card in the display. After a card is examined, it is returned to its proper spot in a protective plastic sheet.

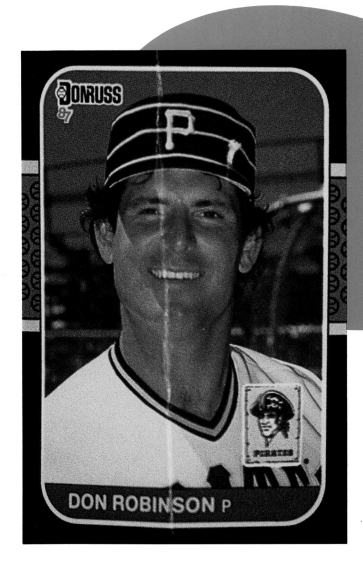

The crease across this 1987 Donruss card may not seem like much, but it's a card-collector's nightmare. A catastrophic defect, this brings the card's value down to zero.

**Fair:** Having one catastrophic defect, such as badly deteriorated border edges and corners, cuts, scratches, holes, or discoloration throughout the card. A card in this condition has been seriously damaged.

**Poor:** (The lowest rated condition for a card.) Having several catastrophic defects. With little value, these cards usually just fill an empty place in a collection until a card in better condition can be found.

Most collectors cringe when they think of cards in the "fair" or "poor" categories. All it takes, however, is one spilled glass of pop or one stray fingernail to turn a near mint prize into an ugly, poor-quality embarrassment. Every collector needs to learn how to protect a good card from bad accidents.

**10**

This ordinary shoebox is a torture chamber for baseball cards. Any card unlucky enough to land in here will be bumped, scraped, bent, and beaten so badly that most collectors don't even want to think about it.

# *Beyond* the *Shoebox*

## How to Store Your Cards

Storing baseball cards is easy, right? You just toss them into a shoebox— or bind them together with a rubber band and throw them in a drawer.

No, no! Don't do it!

Those methods, even though they were once very common, are deadly to your cards. They practically ensure that your cards will warp, bend, get scratched, and wind up with cottony edges.

A baseball card is made of layered paper, a product derived from wood pulp. A somewhat thick middle layer is sandwiched between thinner cover layers—the surfaces on which the photo and the player facts are printed.

Because a card is just ink on paper, it faces many dangers. For one thing, the wood pulp used in making the paper contains an acid, a chemical that will eventually destroy the card by eating away at the fibers of the paper. For another, ultraviolet rays from sunlight or fluorescent lights can fade a card's colors. Also, high humidity can cause a card to swell, and low humidity will cause it to contract. This cycle of swelling and contracting will eventually make the card go limp. Big changes in temperature can have a similar effect.

Sounds pretty awful, doesn't it? In a strict sense, the perfect conditions for storing baseball cards occur only in an airtight, temperature-controlled chamber where sunlight can't enter and where the humidity is always between 50 and 60 percent. That's the kind of chamber used by museums to store precious documents.

So what is a card collector supposed to do? How many of you own an airtight, temperature-controlled chamber? Even if you did, would you want to keep your cards there, sealed away where you could never read them? Baseball cards, after all, are meant to be sorted, read, displayed, traded, and enjoyed.

A sealable plastic bag can be a safe way to store your cards until you get proper plastic sheets. At least it can protect the card from drastic changes in humidity. Such bags, however, should be used only for temporary storage. And never load 15 or 20 cards into a single bag.

Plastic sheets with individual card pockets are very popular among collectors. The sheets can be kept together in three-ring binders.

Fortunately, you *can* protect your cards and enjoy them too.

Clear plastic sheets with card-sized pockets can protect cards from excessive humidity and dust while still permitting you to see both sides of each card. These sheets can be stored in three-ring binders for easy handling. These binders, with their opaque covers, keep sunlight from reaching the cards while the binder is closed. Because each card is in its own pocket, the edges and surfaces of the cards are protected from scratches and wear.

Some experts point out that plastic vinyl—the material of which some plastic sheets are made—will give off a gas that can cause damage to your cards. This gas combines with moisture in the air to produce small amounts of hydrochloric acid, which then eats away at the fibers of the card. To avoid any damage by such acid, you should store your cards in sheets made of some other type of plastic—such as Mylar, polypropylene, or polyethylene.

Don't let those long names scare you. Just remember to avoid plastic vinyl. To find out whether a certain type of card-storage sheet contains plastic vinyl, check the label or ask the manager of the store that sells those sheets. Even though other types of plastic are slightly more expensive than plastic vinyl, the little extra expense buys a lot of extra safety for your cards.

If you would rather not use plastic sheets at all, other methods of storage are reasonably safe. Cardboard boxes made just for card storage come in a variety of sizes—some big enough to hold 3,000 cards. But don't buy a size that is far too big for your collection. If you do, your cards will be sliding around in the box and will get just as tattered as if they had been sliding around in a shoebox.

Individual plastic envelopes made especially for cards are a safe storage tool. They are easy to hold and to pass around.

Make sure that the storage boxes you buy have smooth surfaces, with no little nubs or creases that would damage your cards. It would be horrible to have your cards scratched or bent by the very box that was supposed to protect them. Also, be careful when you take cards out of the box or put them back in. Don't rub cards against one another any more than you have to, and *never* use force to fit them back in the box. If you have to force cards in, it's time to buy another box. Finally, keep the box in a cool, dry place.

Your cards need to be protected. Still, valuable as they are, your cards should also be enjoyed. You can keep a card in fine condition even if you touch it now and then. A reasonable amount of care is all it takes.

A cardboard box made especially for cards is a pretty safe storage place. Try filling any big empty space with a clean, soft cloth until you have enough cards to fill the box. Otherwise, your cards might slide around and get damaged.

**11**

If your parents collected baseball cards when they were kids, they might have some hints for you as you start building your own collection.

# From *Generation* to *Generation*

Card collecting wasn't as serious in the 1950s and 1960s as it is in the 1990s. No monthly price guides. No huge card shows. No museum-style storage techniques. In those days, if you had a double that you couldn't trade, you taped it to your bicycle to make a whirring noise in the spokes as you rode. Even the cards you did keep were just stored in a shoebox.

Parents feel a mixture of emotions when they watch their sons or daughters start card collections. The pleasant feelings might include memories of their own first card collections and their own favorite players. With less pleasure, these parents might remember how badly they beat up their cards or how many really good cards they simply lost.

Many parents wish they had been more careful with their cards. With a baseball card, you have a little cardboard slice of history. Looking at a single image of a baseball player on matted cardboard can let loose a flood of memories—trading cards, talking baseball, the sound of a player's name announced over the radio, the smell of hot dogs at the ballpark.

Saving a piece of baseball history and being able to show it to your kids is fun. Some parents even get special enjoyment out of contributing an old card to a son's or daughter's collection, just to help get the collection started.

Several people in your family might enjoy collecting baseball cards. Your mom or your dad might even have some doubles of classic cards that they want to trade away.

It can also work the other way around. Give your dad or mom a new card as a birthday present or on some other special occasion. It's a great way to get them talking about their own memories of baseball and baseball cards. If your mom and dad still like collecting cards, they might even want to do some trading with you and your friends.

Many of you young collectors of the 1990s will be parents someday too. With any luck—and with proper care—your cards will still be around. You will haul out that Steve Avery rookie card, or that Nolan Ryan 5,000th-strikeout card, or that Cecil Fielder sophomore card. You will show it to your kids and tell the story of how you bought it or traded for it. And then you will really have something special.

The right card at the right price. The satisfaction of filling a gap in your grand slam collection makes all the careful searching worthwhile.

# Index

Kirby Puckett, premier outfielder for the Minnesota Twins, on his 1991 Topps card

# The **Collecting Made Easy** series
## *First steps toward first-class collections*

ACKNOWLEDGMENTS: The publisher gratefully acknowledges the sources of the photographs reproduced in this book: p. 7, General Mills Archives; pp. 8, 9, 14, 15, 16, 17, 18, 21, 23, 24, 25, 26, 28, 30, 36 (right), 38, 41, 47, 49, 50, 51, 54, 58, 64, Lori Schatschneider/Courtesy of J & K Sport Cards, Jeff Margolis and Ken Pritchett; pp. 12, 13, 29, 40, 56, Lori Schatschneider/Courtesy of Jim Kelly; pp. 19, 52, Lori Schatschneider/Courtesy of Krause Publications; pp. 34, 44, Lori Schatschneider/Reproduced with permission of *Beckett Baseball Card Monthly*, 4887 Alpha Road, Suite 200, Dallas, TX 75244; pp. 20, 33, 35, 37, 43, 46, 48, 55, 57, 59, 61, Colleen Sexton; p. 10, National Baseball Library, Cooperstown, New York; p. 22, Minnesota Twins; p. 27, Seattle Mariners; pp. 31, 32, 42, 45, 53, Maria Kaiser; p. 36 (left), Detroit Tigers.

For their kind assistance, the author and the publisher also thank the Fleer Corporation, the Topps Company, Inc., the Upper Deck Company, Leaf, Inc., and the Huberty family (Jim, Mary, Tim, Casey, and Danny) and their friend Jason.